THE WORLD AROUND YOU

OPPOSITES
AT THE ZOO

by
Christianne Jones

PEBBLE
a capstone imprint

Published by Pebble, an imprint of Capstone
1710 Roe Crest Drive, North Mankato, Minnesota 56003
capstonepub.com

Library of Congress Cataloging-in-Publication Data
Names: Jones, Christianne C., author. Title: Opposites at the zoo / by Christianne Jones. Description: North Mankato : Pebble, [2022] | Series: The world around you | Audience: Ages 5-8 | Audience: Grades K-1 | Summary: "Big, stomping elephants. Small, colorful birds. Tall, spotted giraffes. Short, waddling penguins. Opposites are all around at the zoo! This picture book brings opposites from the zoo to young children with interactive, rhyming text and bright photographs"—Provided by publisher. Identifiers: LCCN 2021028241 (print) | LCCN 2021028242 (ebook) | ISBN 9781663976642 (hardcover) | ISBN 9781666326352 (paperback) | ISBN 9781666326369 (ebook pdf) | ISBN 9781666326383 (kindle edition) Subjects: LCSH: Polarity—Juvenile literature. | Zoo animals—Juvenile literature. | English language—Synonyms and antonyms—Juvenile literature. Classification: LCC B830.5 .J66 2022 (print) | LCC B830.5 (ebook) | DDC 146/.7--dc23 LC record available at https://lccn.loc.gov/2021028241 LC ebook record available at https://lccn.loc.gov/2021028242

Editorial Credits
Editor: Christianne Jones; Designer: Brann Garvey; Media Researcher: Svetlana Zhurkin; Production Specialist: Laura Manthe

Image Credits
Shutterstock: Arif Alakbar, 12, Baldreich, (giraffe) 29, bimserd, (gorilla) 28, Deimos91, 16, Denis Tabler, 25, Erick Tessier, (rhino) 28, ex0rzist, (panda) 28, GOLFX, (zebra) 28, Hinochika, 23, Independent birds, 27, Jamie Carroll, 20, Jearu, (lemur) 29, Justin Dawson, 22, Kletr, (chimps) 29, M-Production, (flamingo) 29, Maciej Kopaniecki, 19, Marcel Brekelmans, 13, Minth Fah, 17, N.Minton, (polar near) 29, Natali Glado, (cocktail) 29, NDAB Creativity, 15, Nenad Nedomacki, 18, Nicola Simeoni, 6, Nordic Moonlight, bottom Cover, Richard A Wall, (koala) 29, Riekus, 21, saran.wheel.v, 14, seasoning_17, 24, Somni4uk, 9, Sunti, 7, The Escape of Malee, 26, tratong, (hippo) 29, Trong Nguyen, 3, val lawless, (turtle) 29, Victor Soares, 8, Worakit Sirijinda, top Cover, worldswildlifewonders, 11, Yair Leibovich, (tiger) 28

Special thanks to Sveta Zhurkin and Dan Nunn for their consulting work and help.

Printed and bound in the United States of America. PO4608

OPPOSITES ALL AROUND

Look up high. Look down low.
Opposites surround you
everywhere you go!
Take a trip to the fun-filled zoo,
and discover opposites all around you!

OPPOSITES OVERLOAD

big
and
small

heavy
and
light

old
and
young

fast
and
slow

shallow
and
deep

hot
and
cold

tall
and
short

wet
and
dry

loud
and
quiet

soft
and
hard

day
and
night

What animals will you see in this book?

Turn the page and take a look!

BIG and SMALL

This lumbering elephant is **BIG** and wise.

This attentive meerkat is **SMALL** in size.

LIGHT and **HEAVY**

This **LIGHT** cockatoo perches on a limb.

This **HEAVY** hippo heads for a swim.

YOUNG and OLD

A **YOUNG** and an **OLD** koala cuddle in a tree. It is an adorable moment for visitors to see!

SLOW and FAST

This **SLOW** sloth hangs and sways.

This **FAST** cheetah runs and plays.

SHALLOW and DEEP

These flamingoes in **SHALLOW** water put on a colorful show.

Creatures of all sizes lurk in the **DEEP** water below.

HOT and COLD

This lion rests in the shade on a **HOT** summer day.

These penguins prefer the **COLD** to play.

TALL and SHORT

This **TALL** giraffe takes a break to eat.

This **SHORT** little otter cools off from the heat.

DRY and WET

This **DRY** camel paces around a sandy path.

This **WET** polar bear enjoys a chilly bath.

LOUD and QUIET

This **LOUD** howler monkey is hard to ignore,

unlike the **QUIET** koi fish by the pond's shore.

HARD and SOFT

This tortoise's **HARD** shell gives it extra style.

The alpacas' **SOFT** fur makes everyone smile.

These hanging bats are quite a sight.

They sleep all **DAY** and fly at **NIGHT**!

NAME THE OPPOSITE QUIZ

1. A rhino is **HEAVY**.

What is opposite of heavy?

2. A tiger can be **LOUD**.

What is the opposite of loud?

3. A gorilla is **BIG**.

What is the opposite of big?

4. Zebras like **HOT** weather.

What is the opposite of hot.

5. A panda has **SOFT** fur.

What is the opposite of soft?

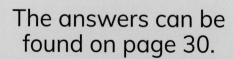

The answers can be
found on page 30.

OPPOSITE OPTIONS QUIZ

Some of these photographs are opposites
and some are not. Can you spot the opposites?

1. **Small** and **Shallow**

2. **Tall** and **Wet**

3. **Old** and **Young**

4. **Happy** and **Mad**

5. **Asleep** and **Awake**

The answers can be found on page 30.

NAME THE OPPOSITE QUIZ ANSWERS

1. The opposite of **HEAVY** is **LIGHT**.
2. The opposite of **LOUD** is **QUIET**.
3. The opposite of **BIG** is **SMALL**.
4. The opposite of **HOT** is **COLD**.
5. The opposite of **SOFT** is **HARD**.

OPPOSITE OPTIONS QUIZ ANSWERS

1. The birds are small. The flamingoes are in shallow water. **Small** and **shallow** are not opposites.
2. The giraffe is tall. The polar bear is wet. **Tall** and **wet** are not opposites.
3. The big tortoise is old. The little tortoise is young. **Old** and **young** are opposites.
4. The two chimpanzees are happy. The hippo is mad. **Happy** and **mad** are opposites.
5. The koala is asleep. The lemur is awake. **Asleep** and **awake** are opposites.

There are lots of opposites.

Here are some additional pairs:

top and **bottom**

above and **below**

front and **back**

out and **in**

light and **dark**

stop and **go**

empty and **full**

closed and **open**

Can you think of any other opposites?

LOOK FOR THE OTHER BOOKS IN THE WORLD AROUND YOU SERIES!

 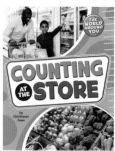   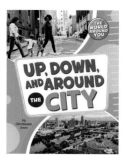

AUTHOR BIO

Christianne Jones has read about a bazillion books, written more than 70, and edited about 1,000. Christianne works as a book editor and lives in Mankato, Minnesota, with her husband and three daughters.